TABLE OF CONTENTS

TIMES ARE CHANGING

Things change over time. Life today is different from the past.

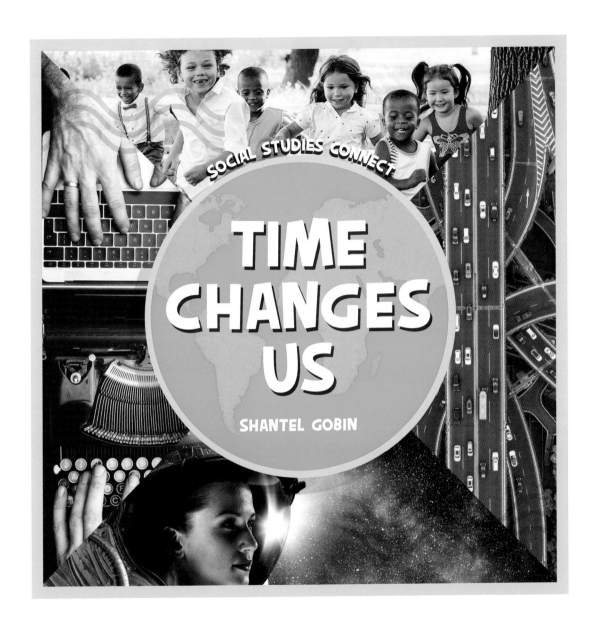

SOCIAL STUDIES CONNECT

TIME CHANGES US

SHANTEL GOBIN

Rourke

SCHOOL to HOME
BEFORE AND DURING READING ACTIVITIES

Before Reading: *Building Background Knowledge and Vocabulary*

Building background knowledge can help children process new information and build upon what they already know. Before reading a book, it is important to tap into what children already know about the topic. This will help them develop their vocabulary and increase their reading comprehension.

Questions and Activities to Build Background Knowledge:

1. Look at the front cover of the book and read the title. What do you think this book will be about?
2. What do you already know about this topic?
3. Take a book walk and skim the pages. Look at the table of contents, photographs, captions, and bold words. Did these text features give you any information or predictions about what you will read in this book?

Vocabulary: *Vocabulary Is Key to Reading Comprehension*

Use the following directions to prompt a conversation about each word.
- Read the vocabulary words.
- What comes to mind when you see each word?
- What do you think each word means?

Vocabulary Words:

- *diverse*
- *evolving*
- *future*
- *technology*

During Reading: *Reading for Meaning and Understanding*

To achieve deep comprehension of a book, children are encouraged to use close reading strategies. During reading, it is important to have children stop and make connections. These connections result in deeper analysis and understanding of a book.

Close Reading a Text

During reading, have children stop and talk about the following:
- Any confusing parts
- Any unknown words
- Text to text, text to self, text to world connections
- The main idea in each chapter or heading

Encourage children to use context clues to determine the meaning of any unknown words. These strategies will help children learn to analyze the text more thoroughly as they read.

When you are finished reading this book, turn to the last page for **After-Reading** activities.

What will life look like in the **future**?

IT'S GO TIME

Long ago, many people traveled by horse and buggy.

Can you imagine life without the cars we have today?

TECH TALK

Cars used to run only on gas. Today, people can buy electric cars that plug into chargers. No gas is needed!

Full steam ahead! We used to hop on steamboats to get around.

8

Today, we can hop on airplanes to travel.

At one time, only astronauts went into outer space. Today, people can pay for a ride into space.

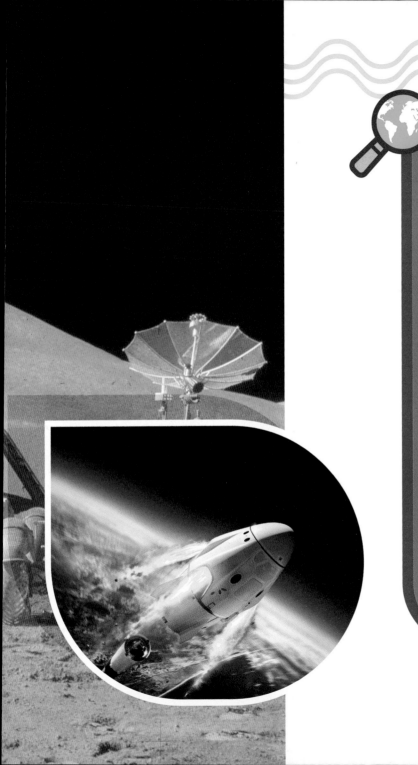

DID YOU KNOW?

A teenager blasted off in a rocket in 2021 on one of the first private trips to outer space.

IT'S SHOWTIME

In the past, families listened to the radio for news and entertainment.

Today, we can watch television.
TV was invented almost
100 years ago.

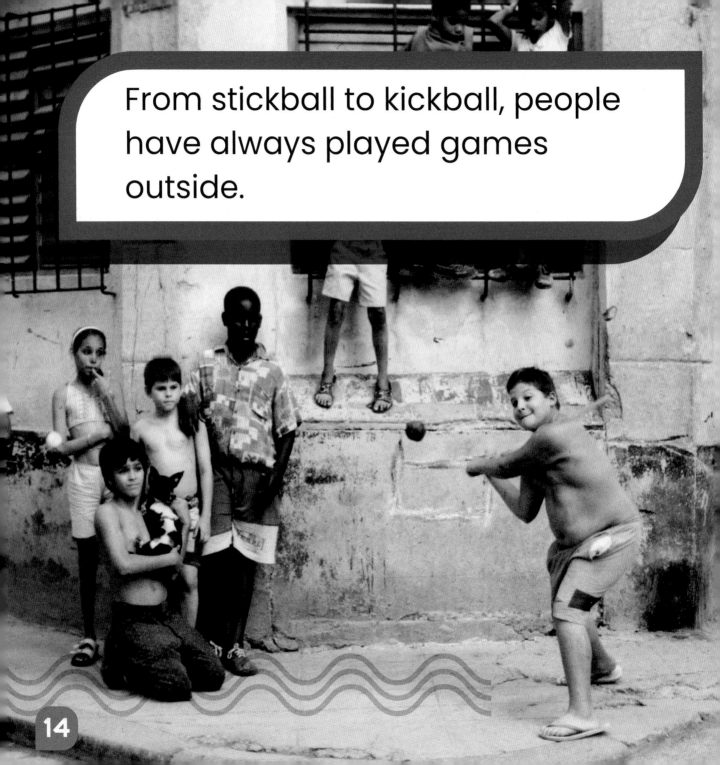

From stickball to kickball, people have always played games outside.

When video games became popular in the 1970s, more people stayed inside to play.

Fun is still **evolving**.

Today, friends can connect to each other around the world with just a click or a tap.

TECH TALK

People started using the internet at home, at work, and at school in the early 1990s. Ten years later, social media sites started popping up.

IT'S GROW TIME

Before settlers arrived, Indigenous peoples lived in much of the United States.

Many were unfairly forced to move from their natural lands. Today, towns and cities grow almost everywhere.

TECH TALK

The telephone was invented in the 1870s. This **technology** helped cities grow fast.

The United States is a **diverse** country. People from many different cultures and backgrounds call it home.

DID YOU KNOW?

Kamala Harris, the first female vice president of the United States, has parents from Jamaica and India.

PHOTO GLOSSARY

diverse (di-VURS): having many different types or kinds

evolving (i-VAHLV-ing): changing slowly or naturally over time

future (FYOO-chur): the time yet to come

technology (tek-NAH-luh-jee): the use of science and engineering to make things

ACTIVITY

"CAN YOU HEAR ME NOW?" HOMEMADE TELEPHONE

Supplies

2 paper cups   yarn

scissors   sharpened pencil

Directions

1. Using the pencil, poke a hole in the bottom of each paper cup.
2. With the scissors, cut a long piece of yarn.
3. Thread the yarn through the bottom of each cup.
4. Tie a knot at each end of the yarn.
5. Give one end of the telephone to a friend. You hold the other end.
6. Walk away from each other until the yarn is fully stretched.
7. Hold your cup to your mouth and speak while your friend holds their cup to their ear and listens.

Did your homemade telephone work? Could your friend hear you? Try making the string different lengths to see what happens.

INDEX

ABOUT THE AUTHOR

Shantel Gobin is an educator and life-long learner. She enjoys living in Brooklyn, New York. She loves exploring history. It is her goal to learn from the past to build a brighter future!

AFTER-READING ACTIVITY

With a parent, go online and do some research. Explore how technology has changed life in the United States over time. What type of technology do you use often? Discuss your research with a family member.

Library of Congress PCN Data

Time Changes Us / Shantel Gobin
(Social Studies Connect)
ISBN 978-1-73165-634-6 (hard cover)(alk. paper)
ISBN 978-1-73165-607-0 (soft cover)
ISBN 978-1-73165-616-2 (eBook)
ISBN 978-1-73165-625-4 (ePub)
Library of Congress Control Number: 2022943006

Rourke Educational Media
Printed in the United States of America
01-0372311937

© 2023 Rourke Educational Media

www.rourkebooks.com

Edited by: Catherine Malaski
Cover design by: Morgan Burnside
Interior design by: Morgan Burnside
Photo Credits: Cover, page 1: ©Sergey Nivens/ Shutterstock.com, ©Rouzes/ Getty Images; Cover, pages 1, 5: ©JaCZhou/ Getty Images; Cover, pages 1, 20-21: ©Kalinovskiy/ Getty Images; page 4: ©rusm/ Getty Images, ©AlenaMozhjer/ Getty Images; page 5: ©ollo/ Getty Images; page 6: ©Cloyne and District Historical Society; page 7: ©Rozhnovskaya Tanya/ Shutterstock.com, ©guteksk7/ Shutterstock.com; page 8: ©ilbusca/ Getty Images; page 9: ©izusek/ Getty Images; pages 10-11: ©National Archives Catalog; page 11: ©Evgeniyqw/ Shutterstock.com, ©BLUE ORIGIN/ UPI/Newscom; page 12: ©FPG/ Getty Images; page 13: ©kali9/ Getty Images, ©Phynart Studio/ Getty Images; page 14: ©Walter Looss; page 15: ©Wikimedia Commons/Creative Commons License,© Serg Novikov/ Shutterstock.com; pages 16-17: ©Ground Picture/ Shutterstock.com; page 17: ©FatCamera/ Getty Images; page 18: ©Wikimedia Commons/ Public Domain, ©bboserup/ Getty Images; page 19: ©Everett Collection/ Shutterstock.com; page 21: ©Michael F. Hiatt/ Shutterstock.com; page 22: ©wavebreakmedia/ Shutterstock.com, ©Dean Clarke/ Shutterstock.com, ©Dilok Klaisataporn. Shutterstock.com, ©Gorodenkoff/ Shutterstock.com